Published by Creative Education
P.O. Box 227, Mankato, Minnesota 56002
Creative Education is an imprint of
The Creative Company
www.thecreativecompany.us

Design by The Design Lab
Production by Chelsey Luther
Art direction by Rita Marshall
Printed in the United States of America

Photographs by Corbis (Frans Lanting), Getty Images
(Richard Du Toit, Art Wolfe), National Geographic
Stock (ELLIOTT NEEP/FLPA/MINDEN PICTURES),
Shutterstock (Amore, iladm, Eric Isselee, Johan
Swanepoel, Ziablik), SuperStock (Animals Animals,
Seth Resnick/Science Faction)

Library of Congress Cataloging-in-Publication Data
Riggs, Kate.
Zebras / Kate Riggs.
p. cm. — (Amazing animals)
Summary: A basic exploration of the appearance,
behavior, and habitat of zebras, the striped African
horses. Also included is a story from folklore explain-
ing how zebras came to have striped fur.
Includes bibliographical references and index.
ISBN 978-1-60818-353-1
1. Zebras—Juvenile literature. I. Title. II. Series:
Amazing animals.

QL737.U62R54 2014
599.665'7—dc23   2013005516

9 8 7 6 5 4 3

ZEBRAS

BY KATE RIGGS

CREATIVE EDUCATION

Zebras are members of the horse family. The three main kinds of zebras live in Africa. Many zebras live in grasslands. They also live in dry, rocky places.

Plains zebras live in countries from Ethiopia to South Africa

Some zebras have "shadow stripes" between the black-and-white stripes

Zebras are known for their striped fur. Every zebra has a different stripe **pattern**. Some kinds of zebras have stripes all the way down their legs. Other zebras have white legs without stripes.

pattern lines or shapes that are repeated

Zebras can be more than five feet (1.5 m) tall at the shoulder. Male zebras are heavier than female zebras. The biggest adult males can weigh up to 1,000 pounds (454 kg). Most adults weigh about 700 pounds (318 kg).

Males are called stallions and females are called mares

*Zebras bark and
make other sounds to
talk to each other*

A zebra is a kind of animal called
a mammal. Mammals have hair or fur.
They feed their young with milk. Zebras
live in hot places. They sweat and **pant**
to cool off.

pant take short, quick breaths

Zebras eat plants. They eat a lot of grass and leaves from small bushes. Zebras have teeth that are good for chewing. A zebra needs to drink water almost every day.

A watering hole is a place where many zebras gather

*Foals can stand up
about 20 minutes
after their birth*

A mother zebra has one **foal**. A foal is born with white fur and brown stripes. It weighs 55 to 88 pounds (25–40 kg). The foal drinks milk from its mother. It starts eating grass when it is about one week old.

foal a baby zebra

A single stallion leads his harem of mares and young

Zebras live in groups called harems, bands, or herds. Bands of zebras usually have many females or many males, but not both. Bands join together to make a zebra herd. A zebra can live for about 25 years in the wild.

harems small groups of zebras that have only one male and many females

Zebras can run 40 miles (64 km) per hour to get away from lions

Groups of zebras feed in the daytime. A male zebra looks out for **predators** like lions and cheetahs. He barks to let other zebras know if a predator is close. Zebras make a circle around their foals to keep them safe.

predators animals that kill and eat other animals

Wild zebras often run into other animals at watering holes

Zebras are popular animals to see at zoos. They can live a long time in a zoo. Some people go to Africa on **safari**. They hope to see many of these striped animals there!

safari a trip to see wild animals in Africa

A *Zebra* Story

Why do zebras not have horns? People in Africa told a story about this. Zebra used to be white with long, dark horns on his head. He made fun of another animal named Oryx. Oryx asked Zebra if he could try on his horns. Then Oryx ran away with them! Zebra chased Oryx but got tangled up in Oryx's baggy, striped coat. Ever since then, zebras have had striped fur but no horns.

Read More

Clutton-Brock, Juliet. *Horse*. New York: DK Publishing, 2008.

Zobel, Derek. *Zebras*. Minneapolis: Bellwether Media, 2012.

Websites

Letter Z Zebra Theme
http://www.first-school.ws/activities/alpha/z/zebra.htm
This site has zebra crafts, worksheets, and coloring pages to print out.

National Geographic Kids Creature Feature: Zebras
http://kids.nationalgeographic.com/kids/animals/creaturefeature/zebra/
This site has pictures and videos of zebras.

Index

Africa 4, 20
foals 15, 19
food 12, 15, 19
fur 7, 11, 15, 22
groups 16, 19
life span 16, 20

mammals 11
predators 19
sizes 8
stripes 7, 15, 20, 22
teeth 12
zoos 20